S E A S O N S

Four Seasons by Marie Taylor

25 YEARS OF PHOTOGRAPHY AT THE MISSOURI BOTANICAL GARDEN BY JACK JENNINGS

INTRODUCTION BY DR. PETER H. RAVEN

For Michiko

First printing 2003

Library of Congress Cataloging in Publication Data

Special thanks to Tim Michels, Aaron Michels, Eddie O'Donnell and Wayne Kissel.

Design and separations by PPI Graphix Inc., St. Louis, Missouri
Printed by Columbine Printing Company.

For more information:
1-800-786-7855
Website: jackjennings.net

Printed in the United States of America

ISBN 0-9742889-0-X

1 2 3 4 5 6 7 8 9 000 2005 2004 2003

Introduction

Other than the real thing, nothing is so splendidly beautiful as Jack Jennings' photographs of the Missouri Botanical Garden and its Shaw Nature Reserve. If only our founder, Henry Shaw, were here to admire Jack's photographs! They have graced the Garden's calendars since the first one appeared in 1982.

Henry Shaw, who emigrated from England and arrived in St. Louis in 1820, envisioned a garden that would provide a common place for St. Louisians to meet, to learn about the importance of plants to their lives, and see the beauty of nature. At this garden, educational programs would inform their children and through research lead to discoveries that would profoundly affect their future and the future of society throughout the world. The Missouri Botanical Garden opened in 1859 and has served the public, fulfilling Shaw's vision, ever since.

Photo by Peter Howard

Jack Jennings began photographing the Missouri Botanical Garden in the summer of 1978. As soon as I saw his work, I was struck by its extraordinary quality and the manner in which his eye captured the essence of the natural scene through the seasons. His images have won numerous awards in regional and world-wide competitions, and have been reproduced in the *National Geographic, Time, Fine Gardening,* the *National Gardener,* and many other garden and nature magazines.

We are very proud of his work, and of the devotion he has shown to his art. In this book he selects a collection of images that reflect the beauty of the Missouri Botanical Garden in each season. We hope that you will find as much joy in it as we do in the Garden itself, and as much as Jack did taking these beautiful photographs.

Dr. Peter H. Raven
Director - Missouri Botanical Garden

1. Ridgway Center, entrance to the Missouri Botanical Garden.

2. Moon gate in the Gladney Rose Garden.

3. Greigii tulip, *Tulipa* 'Red Riding Hood' and Grape hyacinth, *Muscari armeniacum.*

4. Samuels Bulb Garden.

5. Parrot tulips, *Tulipa* 'Texas Gold' at the William T. Kemper Center for Home Gardening.

6. *The Victory of Science Over Ignorance* by Carlo Nicoli.

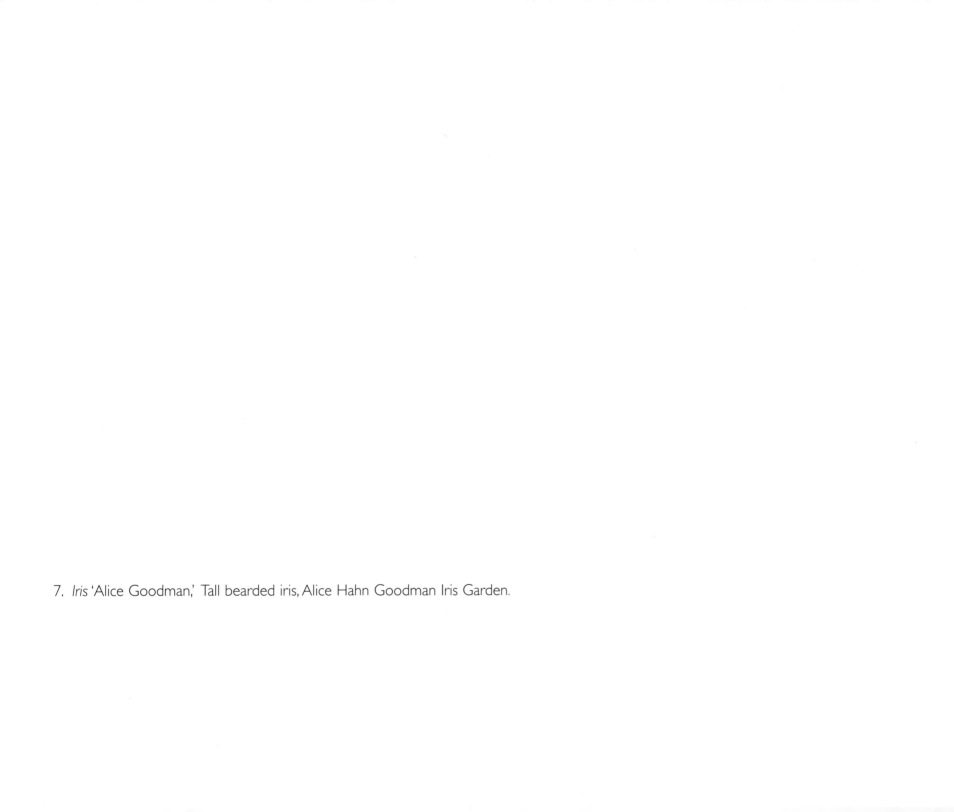

7. *Iris* 'Alice Goodman,' Tall bearded iris, Alice Hahn Goodman Iris Garden.

8. Distant view of Tower Grove House.

9. Bleeding hearts, *Dicentra spectabilis.*

10. The Gate House.

11. Peonies in *Seiwa-en*, the Japanese Garden.

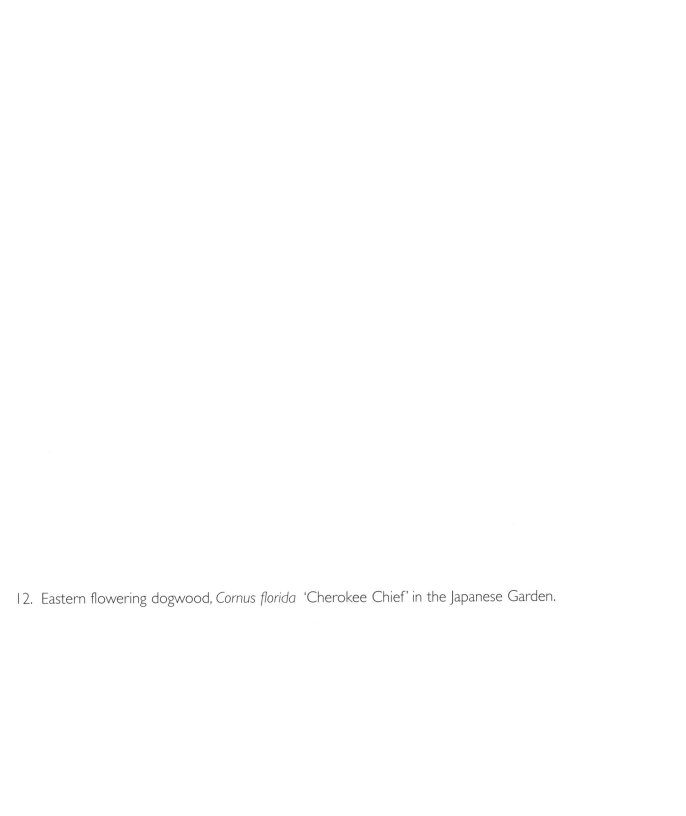

12. Eastern flowering dogwood, *Cornus florida* 'Cherokee Chief' in the Japanese Garden.

13. Weeping higan cherry, *Prunus subhirtella* 'Pendula,' Japanese Garden.

14. Teahouse Island, Japanese Garden.

15. Japanese irises, *Iris ensata*, Japanese Garden.

16. Wetland boardwalk, Shaw Nature Reserve.

17. Dogwood, *Cornus florida*, Shaw Nature Reserve.

18. Stream to the Blue Boulder Cascade, *Segan-no-Take*.

19. Perennial border in the Swift Family Garden.

20. Lily pools in front of the Climatron.

21. Tropical water lily, *Nymphaea* 'Mrs. George C. Hitchcock.'

22. Victoria water lilies.

23. *Hemerocallis* 'Ruby Throat' in the G. Stewart Jenkins Daylily Garden.

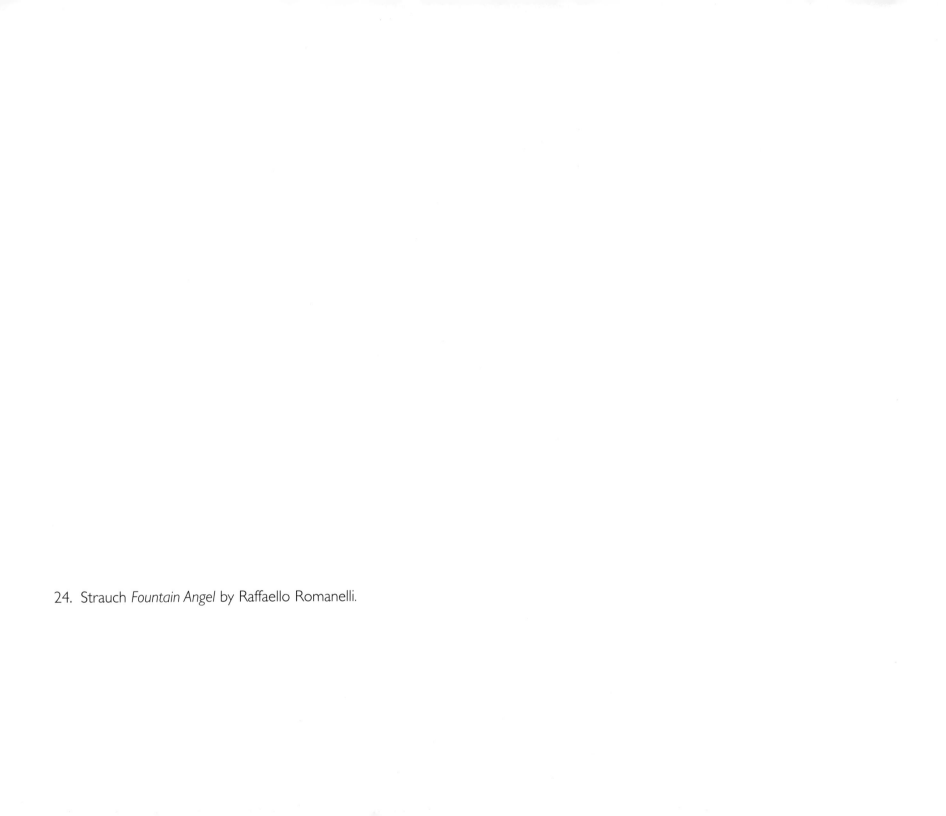

24. Strauch *Fountain Angel* by Raffaello Romanelli.

25. *Caladium* x *bicolor* 'White Queen.'

26. *Idea leuconoe*, the paper kite butterfly, rests on a Peregrina, *Jatropha integerrima*, at the Sophia M. Sachs Butterfly House.

27. Kresko Family Victorian Garden.

28. Floribunda Rose, *Rosa* 'Brass Band' in the Anne L. Lehmann Rose Garden.

29. Shapleigh Fountain.

30. Globe amaranth, *Gomphrena* 'Strawberry Fields' and Black-eyed Susan, *Rudbeckia hirta,* in the Kemper Center for Home Gardening.

31. The Ruth Palmer Blanke Boxwood Garden.

32. Hybrid tea rose, *Rosa* 'Jacnor' SIGNATURE ®.

33. Lotus, *Nelumbo nucifera.*

34. Shapleigh fountain.

Fall

35. Full moon maple, *Acer japonicum* 'Aconitifolium.'

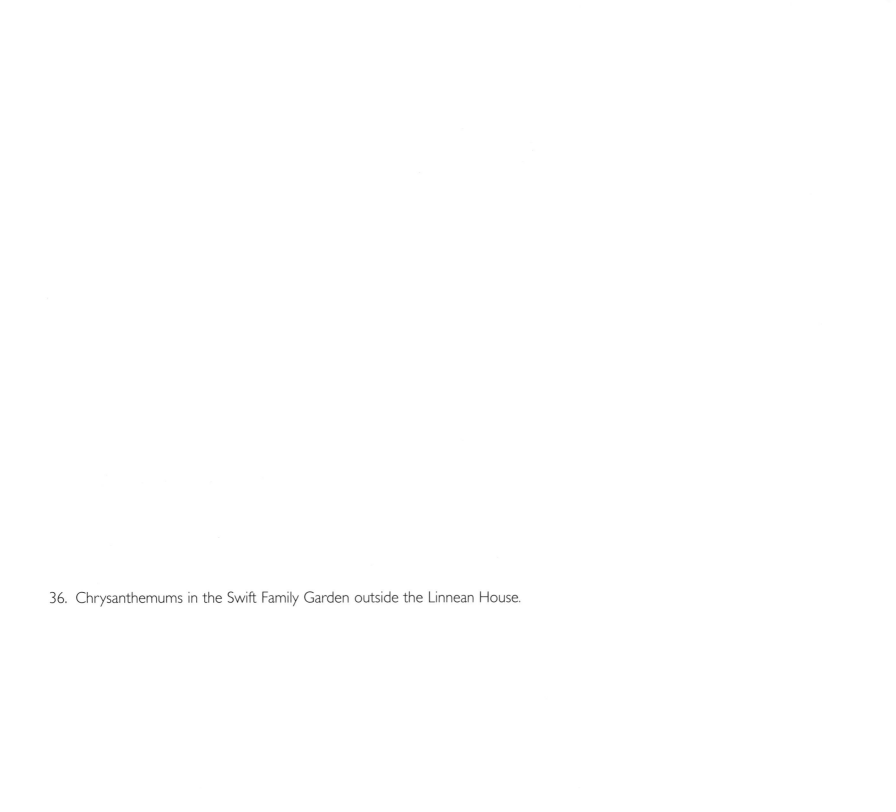

36. Chrysanthemums in the Swift Family Garden outside the Linnean House.

37. *Zerogee* by Paul Theodore Granlund.

38. Elephant ear, *Caladium* x *bicolor* 'Frieda Hemple.'

39. Moon Gate entrance to the Margaret Grigg Nanjing Friendship Garden.

40. Margaret Grigg Nanjing Frienship Garden.

41. Frieze, Margaret Grigg Nanjing Friendship Garden.

42. Oakleaf hydrangea, *Hydrangea quercifolia* 'Snow Queen.'

43. *The Three Graces* by Gerhard Marcks in the English Woodland Garden.

44. Crane Island, Japanese Garden.

45. Koi, *Cyprinus carpio*, Japanese Garden.

46. River birch, *Betula nigra,* Japanese Garden.

47. Tatarian maple, *Acer tataricum*, the Knolls.

48. *The Bather* by Emilio Greco, in front of the Linnean House.

49. *Camellia japonica* 'Claudia Lee' in the Linnean House.

50. Seven bronzes by Carl Milles in front of the Climatron.

51. *Laeliocattleya* hybrid at the annual orchid show.

52. Moorish Garden, Shoenberg Temperate House.

53. Tower Grove House and the Mausoleum Grove.

54. Tower Grove House, the country home of Henry Shaw.

55. Winterberry, *Ilex verticillata* 'Nana' RED SPRITE.

56. Azalea leaves with frost.

57. *Segan-no-take*, the Blue Boulder Cascade, Japanese Garden.

58. *Taikobashi*, the Drum Bridge, Japanese Garden.

59. *Yatsuhashi,* the Zig Zag Bridge, Japanese Garden.

60. Reflections of bald cypresses, *Taxodium distichum*.

61. The Garden's founder: *Henry Shaw*, by Paul Granlund.

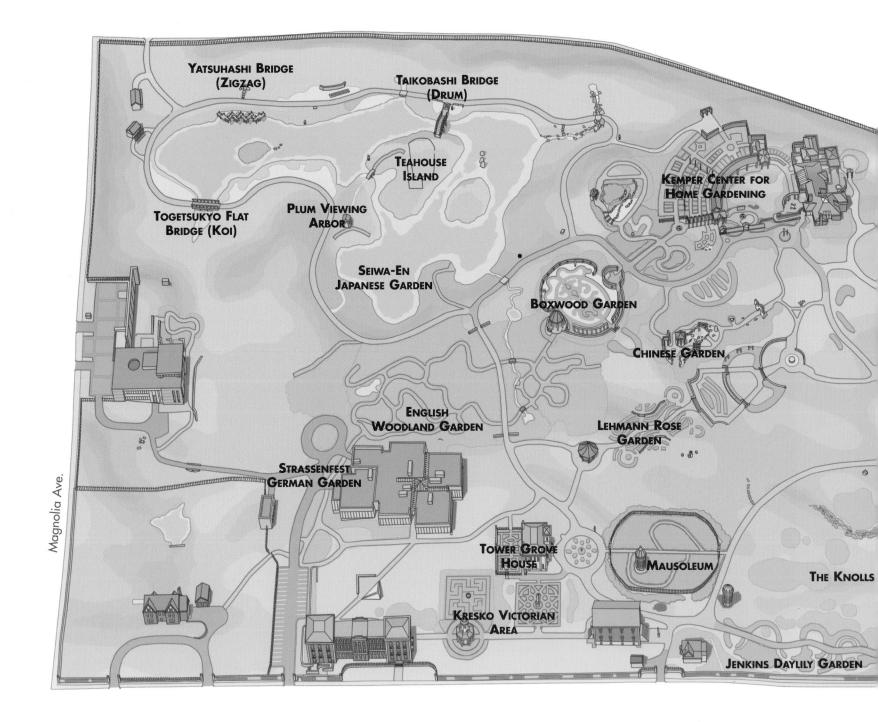

YATSUHASHI BRIDGE (ZIGZAG)

TAIKOBASHI BRIDGE (DRUM)

TEAHOUSE ISLAND

TOGETSUKYO FLAT BRIDGE (KOI)

PLUM VIEWING ARBOR

KEMPER CENTER FOR HOME GARDENING

SEIWA-EN JAPANESE GARDEN

BOXWOOD GARDEN

CHINESE GARDEN

Magnolia Ave.

ENGLISH WOODLAND GARDEN

LEHMANN ROSE GARDEN

STRASSENFEST GERMAN GARDEN

TOWER GROVE HOUSE

MAUSOLEUM

THE KNOLLS

KRESKO VICTORIAN AREA

JENKINS DAYLILY GARDEN